GROWING BAMBOO FOR BEGINNERS

A Step-by-Step Guide to
Successful Bamboo Growing:
From Choosing Varieties,
Planting, Care & Troubleshooting

Joe P. Hayes

Table of Contents

CHAPTER ONE 4
- What is bamboo? 4
- Benefits of Growing Bamboo 6
- Types of Bamboo 10
- Applications for Bamboo 14

CHAPTER TWO 15
- Popular Bamboo Varieties for Beginners 15
- Choosing the Right Bamboo ... 19
- Planting Bamboo 21

CHAPTER THREE 24
- Planting Techniques 24
- Caring for Bamboo 26
- Managing Bamboo Growth 29

CHAPTER FOUR 33
- Controlling Spread of Running Bamboo 33

Troubleshooting Common
  Problems 36
THE END......................................40

CHAPTER ONE
What is bamboo?

Bamboo has deep symbolic meanings in many different contexts and civilizations, and it's frequently connected to qualities like strength, flexibility, and tenacity. The following are some major metaphorical connotations associated with bamboo:

Bamboo is renowned for its ability to bend without breaking, which represents strength and the capacity to face hardship.

Adaptability & Flexibility: Bamboo's flexibility is a symbol of the value that many civilizations place on the capacity to change with the times and go with the flow.

Health and Longevity: Due to

its fast growth and year-round greenness, bamboo is frequently linked to longevity, good health, and immortal youth in Chinese culture.

Purity & Innocence: The straight, upright growth of bamboo is considered a sign of innocence and purity.

Prosperity and Good Fortune: Bamboo is said to infuse a home or place of business with prosperity, good fortune, and positive energy according to Feng Shui.

Humility and Simplicity: Bamboo is a strong material that nevertheless has a modest appearance, signifying humility and simplicity.

Friendship: Because bamboo typically grows in clusters to support one another, it is symbolic of friendship and the strength of interpersonal relationships in several Asian cultures.

Cultural Significance: Bamboo is frequently employed in customary festivities and rituals in Japan, where it is considered a symbol of fortune.

Benefits of Growing Bamboo

There are several advantages to growing bamboo, both financially and environmentally. Here are a few main benefits:

Advantages for the Environment

Carbon Sequestration: Compared to many other plants, bamboo releases more oxygen and absorbs more carbon dioxide, which helps to slow down global warming.

Soil conservation: Bamboo's deep root system stabilizes the soil, reducing soil erosion and enhancing soil health.

Biodiversity: Bamboo plantations support biodiversity by offering a home for a variety of species.

Water Conservation: Bamboo helps keep groundwater levels stable and uses less water than other crops.

Bamboo grows quickly, which makes it an extremely renewable resource. In a single day, several species can grow up to three feet.

Bamboo can help restore land by absorbing and accumulating heavy metals and other contaminants from the soil. This process is known as phytoremediation.

Financial Gains

Versatile Material: Bamboo offers a multitude of economic options due to its vast range of applications, from furniture and construction materials to clothing and paper.

Employment Creation: Growing and processing bamboo can generate employment and stimulate local economies in both urban and rural regions.

Low Maintenance Costs: Compared to other crops, bamboo requires less care after it is planted, which lowers farmers' maintenance expenses.

Sustainable Agriculture: Since bamboo doesn't need to be replanted, it can provide a steady yield, making it a viable source of income.

Potential for Tourism: Bamboo woods have the potential to draw tourists and generate extra cash for nearby towns.

Social Advantages

Community Development: By giving the local populace resources and a source of income, bamboo farming can aid in community development initiatives.

Bamboo possesses traditional and cultural value in numerous cultures, aiding in the preservation of cultural history.

Possibilities for Education: Bamboo plantations can act as teaching grounds for environmentally friendly farming methods and preservation of the environment.

Advantages of Agriculture

Intercropping: By growing bamboo alongside other crops, farmers can maximize their use of land and raise their income.

Bamboo has a natural resistance to a wide range of illnesses and pests, which lowers the need for chemical pesticides.

Climate Resilience: Bamboo is a crop that can withstand harsh weather conditions due to its adaptability to a wide range of climates.

Types of Bamboo

The grass family Poaceae has a varied range of perennial evergreen plants known as bamboo. Bamboo comes in more than 1,400 species, and they are divided into several kinds according to their growth patterns, sizes, and intended applications. Here are a few typical bamboo species:

1. Bamboo Clumping (Sympodial)

<u>Fargesia</u>: Preferred for gardening and landscaping due to its non-invasive growing habit. Fargesia rufa and robusta are two examples.

<u>Bambusa:</u> These are tropical bamboos that are frequently used as ornaments. Bambusa oldhamii (Giant Timber Bamboo) and Bambusa multiplex (Hedge Bamboo) are two examples.

2. Bamboo in motion (monopodial)

<u>Phyllostachys:</u> Often used for building and lumber, this plant is noted for its quick rhizome spread. Phyllostachys aurea, or golden bamboo, and Phyllostachys nigra, or black bamboo, are two examples.

<u>Pleioblastus:</u> Usually smaller, these are frequently utilized as ground cover. Pleioblastus fortunei and Pleioblastus pygmaeus, or dwarf bamboo, are two examples.

3. Wooden Bamboo

<u>Dendrocalamus:</u> A large species utilized in scaffolding and construction. Dendrocalamus giganteus and Dendrocalamus strictus are two examples.

<u>Guadua:</u> Originally from South America, this robust wood is

utilized for construction. One such instance is Guadua angustifolia.

4. Decorative Bamboo

Chimonobambusa: Noted for its eye-catching leaf and stems, this plant is useful as a decoration. Chimonobambusa tumidissinoda and Chimonobambusa quadrangularis are two examples.

Shibataea: A bamboo that grows in gardens that is tiny to medium in size. One such instance is Shibataea kumasaca.

5. Bamboo Ground Cover

Sasa: Shallow, spreading bamboo used for erosion prevention and ground cover. Sasa palmata and Sasa veitchii are two examples.

Indocalamus: Known for its big leaves, this plant is used in landscaping and gardening. One such instance is Indocalamus tessellatus.

6. Massive Bamboo

Gigantochloa: Big bamboos used as ornamental, craft, and lumber. One such instance is Gigantochloa apus.

Melocanna: Contains some of the biggest species of bamboo. One such instance is Melocanna baccifera.

7. Tiny Bamboo

Pleioblastus: Because of its modest size, it is frequently employed as a low ground cover. Pleioblastus pygmaeus and Pleioblastus viridistriatus are two examples.

Pogonatherum: Also referred to as miniature bamboo, this plant is good for indoor and small-scale gardening. Pogonatherum paniceum, or bamboo grass, is one example.

Applications for Bamboo

Phyllostachys, Guadua, and Dendrocalamus for scaffolding and construction.

Bambusa, Fargesia, and Chimonobambusa for ornamental purposes.

Pleioblastus Sasa: Ground Cover and Erosion Control.

Furniture and Crafts: Gigantochloa, Bambusa.

Phyllostachys and Dendrocalamus are edible shoots.

CHAPTER TWO
Popular Bamboo Varieties for Beginners

A few well-liked bamboo kinds that are good for novices are as follows:

Phyllostachys aurea, or golden bamboo:

Features: Noted for its thick foliage and vivid yellow canes. Because it is a clumping bamboo, it grows in close-knit clumps as opposed to widely spreading.

Growing conditions: Well-drained soil and full light are preferred over partial shade. It may require protection from severe winds, but it can withstand a variety of temperatures.

The pseudosasa japonica, or Arrow Bamboo:

Features: Its delicate foliage and slender, green canes give it an elegant appearance. This bamboo grows slowly in clumps.

Growing Conditions: Prefers wet, well-drained soil and partial shade. It is resilient and able to withstand colder weather.

Bamboo giant (Bambusa oldhamii):

Features: One of the bigger bamboos, distinguished by its culms (canes) with thick walls that can grow to considerable heights (up to 55 feet or more).

Growing Conditions*:* Needs lots of water and full sun. It grows in big clumps and is suitable for tropical and subtropical regions.

Varieties of Fargesia (such as Fargesia robusta and Fargesia murielae):

<u>Features</u>: The rich foliage and non-invasive growth tendencies of these clumping bamboos are well-known. It's common to refer to them as "clumping bamboos for cold climates."

<u>Growing Conditions:</u> Prefers regularly moist, well-drained soil with some shade. When compared to many other bamboo species, they are more resilient to cold.

Varieties of dwarf bamboo (Pleioblastus):

<u>Features:</u> Bamboo species that spread slowly and are good for ground cover or container gardening. They can be highly decorative and have tiny leaves.

Growing conditions: Regular watering and partial shade are preferred. Certain types are able to withstand lower temperatures.

Choosing the Right Bamboo

Selecting the ideal bamboo for your garden requires taking the soil's requirements and environment into account.

Considering the climate

Hardiness Zone: The ability of bamboo species to withstand cold varies. Select a species that is appropriate for the local climate zone or your USDA hardiness zone. While certain bamboos (such the Phyllostachys species) are more suited to warmer regions, others are more cold-hardy and can survive below freezing temperatures.

Sunlight: Full sun is preferred by most bamboo species over partial shade. Select a bamboo species that is appropriate for the amount of sunlight your garden receives.

Humidity: Although certain species are better suited to drier climes, bamboo generally loves damp environments. Choose a species of bamboo that can withstand low humidity if that's where you reside.

Conditions for Soil:

Bamboo likes its soil to drain well. Steer clear of soils that are wet all the time, as this might cause root rot. Composted organic matter can be added to thick clay soil to improve drainage.

pH Level: Generally speaking,

bamboo prefers slightly acidic soil (pH 6.0–7.0) over neutral soil. Find out what pH your soil is by conducting a soil test, then select a bamboo species that grows well in that pH range.

Fertility: Rich soil is ideal for bamboo growth. Before planting, adding organic matter—such as compost or well-rotted manure—will increase soil fertility and supply vital nutrients for strong, healthy growth.

Planting Bamboo

Planting bamboo can be a gratifying project, but to ensure success, it's critical to select the ideal location and use the right planting procedures. This is a handbook to assist you:

Site Selection

<u>Climate and Hardiness:</u> The hardiness and climate preferences of different bamboo types vary. Select a species that is appropriate for the climate in your area.

<u>Sunlight:</u> Although some varieties may withstand slight shade, most bamboos require full sun. Make sure the location is receiving enough sunshine in accordance with the needs of the bamboo species.

<u>Soil:</u> Rich in organic matter and well-drained, bamboo grows in this type of soil. It likes soil that is slightly acidic (pH 6.0–7.0) as opposed to neutral.

When choosing a planting location for bamboo, take into account the species' mature size. Plants should be spaced appropriately to promote healthy development without being overcrowded.

<u>Water:</u> Bamboo requires consistent irrigation, particularly in the early stages of growth. Make sure there is irrigation or water available for the site.

CHAPTER THREE
Planting Techniques
Getting the Soil Ready:

Create a hole that is twice as broad as the bamboo plant's root ball.

To increase the soil's fertility and drainage, add compost or well-rotted manure.

Planting:

The bamboo plant should be positioned in the middle of the hole at the same depth as it was in the nursery or container.

To eliminate any air pockets, carefully compact the earth surrounding the roots as you backfill the hole.

Watering

As soon as you plant, give the soil surrounding the roots a good watering.

Maintain a constant moisture content in the soil, particularly in the first year following planting.

Mulching:

Mulch the area surrounding the plant's base to help it retain moisture and keep weeds at bay. Additionally, mulch insulates the roots.

Assistance (if required):

Staking or other forms of support may be beneficial for certain types of bamboo until they develop strong roots and are able to stand straight.

Upkeep:

Keep a close eye on the bamboo's water requirements, particularly in the dry months.

To promote healthy growth, fertilize bamboo plants once a year in the spring with a balanced fertilizer.

Caring for Bamboo

Pruning, general maintenance, fertilization, and watering are some of the most important parts of bamboo care. Here is a how-to for each:

Applying fertilizer and water

Watering

Frequency: Bamboo usually needs to be watered on a frequent basis, especially in the dry months. Make sure the soil is constantly damp but not soggy.

Watering thoroughly will promote the growth of deeply rooted plants. Weak root systems may result from shallow irrigation.

To assess the moisture content of the soil, insert your finger into it; it should feel damp but not soaked.

Getting fertilized

Frequency: During the growing season (spring and summer), bamboo usually benefits from routine fertilizing.

Apply a balanced fertilizer (such 10-10-10 or something similar) or one made especially for bamboo.

Application: Apply fertilizer around the base of the plant, paying attention to the amount recommendations on the package. Don't overfertilize because too much fertilizer can cause bamboo to become sensitive.

Maintenance and Pruning

Reduction:

The goal of pruning is to keep bamboo in its natural shape, get rid of any damaged or dead canes, and limit its spread.

<u>Tools</u>: For thicker canes, use a saw or a pair of sharp pruning shears.

When new shoots appear, prune bamboo in late spring or early summer. Pruning should be avoided in the fall and winter since it can leave the plant susceptible to cold harm.

<u>Method:</u> To remove canes, cut them at the base. To increase

ventilation, thin down dense growth and trim back any undesirable shoots.

Upkeep:

Containment: Subterranean rhizomes allow bamboo to spread quickly. To stop bamboo from spreading, think about growing it in containers or using obstacles (such as rhizome barriers).

Check plants frequently for indications of pests (such as aphids or spider mites) or diseases (such as fungal infections). If discovered, take quick action.

Winter maintenance: Certain bamboo species are susceptible to the cold. Mulch the base of plants in colder climates to shield the roots from freezing temperatures.

Managing Bamboo Growth

Because bamboo is known to spread quickly and occasionally indiscriminately, managing its development can be crucial. The following advice can be used to control bamboo growth:

Physical barriers composed of metal or high-density polyethylene (HDPE) can be used to contain bamboo. To stop the spread of underground rhizomes, these barriers should be buried around the edge of the bamboo grove at least eighteen inches deep.

<u>Rhizome Pruning:</u> To stop subterranean rhizomes from expanding beyond of intended bounds, examine and trim them on a regular basis. To cut and remove rhizomes that are invading unwelcome places, use a sharp

shovel or spade.

<u>Maintenance</u>: If new shoots get too dense, they should be thinned out. Old and dead culms (stalks) should be removed on a regular basis. This aids in managing the bamboo grove's general growth and look.

<u>Selecting Clumping variants:</u> Running variants are not as good for planting bamboo as clumping varieties. Because they spread slowly and form compact clusters, clumping bamboos are simpler to maintain.

<u>Chemical reduce:</u> Herbicides containing imazapyr or glyphosate might be used as a last option to reduce bamboo growth. This approach should only be taken cautiously and in situations when alternative approaches are

unfeasible or unworkable.

<u>Frequent Monitoring:</u> Pay special attention to the bamboo grove and note any changes in its growth. If you see dense growth or spreading rhizomes early on, you can control the bamboo more effectively.

CHAPTER FOUR
Controlling Spread of Running Bamboo

Although stopping the spread of flowing bamboo can be difficult, there are a few practical strategies you can use:

Physical Barriers: To stop the bamboo's rhizomes (underground stems) from spreading outside of the specified area, install a strong physical barrier around the perimeter that is at least 2 feet (60 cm) deep into the earth. Make use of materials like metal barriers or high-density polyethylene (HDPE) that are intended especially for containing bamboo.

Root Pruning: Using a sharp spade or other pruning instrument, regularly trim any rhizomes that straddle the intended region. Considering how quickly bamboo can spread, this strategy calls for attention and regular observation.

<u>Maintenance of the Rhizome Barrier:</u> Every year, inspect the barrier to make sure there are no openings or other damage that can let bamboo rhizomes escape. As needed, replace or repair the barrier.

<u>Mowing and Edging:</u> By regularly trimming back new growth before it becomes established, the boundaries of the bamboo grove can help keep the plants under control.

<u>Chemical inhibit:</u> Herbicides containing glyphosate or imazapyr can be sprayed directly to cut rhizomes or to leaves to inhibit bamboo growth in circumstances

where manual approaches are not feasible or effective. When using herbicides, always make sure you follow the manufacturer's instructions and any local laws.

Containment Pots: You can stop the spread of bamboo by planting it in big, robust pots or containers. Select containers with substantial walls to stop rhizomes from penetrating.

Watch for New Shoots: Keep an eye out for any new shoots that might appear in the bamboo grove that are not part of the approved zone. Remove these shoots as soon as possible to stop their spread.

Speak with a Professional: A professional landscaper or bamboo specialist can offer customized guidance and support if you're unclear about the ideal way to manage bamboo in your particular circumstances.

Troubleshooting Common Problems

Depending on what you're working with, there are many different approaches you can take when troubleshooting common issues, but here are some general ones:

<u>Determine the Issue:</u> Clearly state what the problem is. Is there a software bug (like a program crashing), a hardware problem (like a device not working), or anything else?

<u>assemble Information:</u> Compile specifics regarding the issue. When did it begin? Has there been any recent change (such as

updates or fresh installations)? Which error messages or symptoms are present?

Restart: By restarting the system and ending any problematic processes, a simple restart can resolve a lot of problems.

Verify Connections: In order to rule out hardware problems, make that all connectors, wires, and plugs are safe and in good working order.

Update Software: Ensure that the drivers, programs, and operating system on your computer are current. Updates frequently come with improvements and problem fixes.

Examine for Viruses and Malware: To rule out malicious software causing problems, perform an antivirus software scan.

Make Space: Performance problems may arise from insufficient disk space. Remove files that aren't needed or transfer them to an external drive.

Inspect for overheating: Hardware issues may arise from overheating. Verify that the device's fans are operating, the vents are clear, and it isn't overheating.

Examine Recent Changes: If the issue arose following a recent change (such as installing new software or updates), you may want to investigate rolling back those changes or seeing if there are any known problems associated with them.

Hardware Diagnostics: To check for problems with hardware

components, use third-party software or the built-in diagnostic tools.

Restore to a Previous State: To return your system to a previous stable state, use Time Machine on a Mac or System Restore on Windows.

Seek Support: Try searching support forums, getting in touch with your device or software's customer service, or hiring a professional specialist if you can't figure out the problem on your own.

THE END

www.ingramcontent.com/pod-product-compliance
Lightning Source LLC
Chambersburg PA
CBHW030100230526
45471CB00003B/1181